Fingerpower®
Level Five

Effective Technic for All Piano Methods
By John W. Schaum

FOREWORD

Strong fingers are an important requirement for all pianists, amateur and professional. Schaum Fingerpower® exercises are designed to strengthen all five fingers of both hands. Equal hand development is assured by the performance of the same patterns in each hand. The exercises are short and easily memorized. This enables the student to focus his/her efforts on technical benefits, listening attentively and playing with a steady beat.

To derive the full benefit of these exercises, careful attention must be given to how they are practiced. They should be played with a firm, solid finger action. The student must listen carefully during practice. It is important to be aware of the feeling in the fingers and hands while playing. The student should try to play each finger equally loud. Each hand should also be equally loud.

The exercises become progressively more difficult as the student moves through the book. This makes the exercises an ideal companion to a method book at the same level.

The series consists of seven books, Primer Level through Level 6.

Practice CD's and MIDI diskettes with orchestrated accompaniments are available for Primer Level through Level 4. They promote accurate playing with a steady rhythm, while making practice more enjoyable. MIDI diskettes have separate tracks for right hand, left hand, harmony, bass and rhythm.

Schaum Publications, Inc.
10235 N. Port Washington Rd. • Mequon, WI 53092
www.schaumpiano.net

© Copyright 1970 by Schaum Publications, Inc., Mequon, Wisconsin
International Copyright Secured • All Rights Reserved • Printed in U.S.A.
ISBN-13: 978-1-936098-36-1

EXCLUSIVELY DISTRIBUTED BY

HAL•LEONARD®
CORPORATION
7777 W. BLUEMOUND RD. P.O. BOX 13819 MILWAUKEE, WI 53213

04-25

CONTENTS

Exercise	Page
1. Finger Repetition Study	3
2. Melody and Accompaniment	4
3. Accompaniment and Melody	5
4. Modulation (chords)	6
5. Modulation (arpeggios)	6
6. Legato Sixths	8
7. Diatonic Octaves	9
8. Broken Octaves (ascending)	10
9. Broken Octaves (descending)	11
10. Tremolo (sustained octaves)	12

Exercise	Page
11. Tremolo (sustained thirds)	13
12. Parallel Arpeggios	14
13. Arpeggios in Contrary Motion	15
14. Sustained Octaves (repeated thirds)	16
15. Sustained Thirds (repeated octaves)	17
16. Three Octave Arpeggios (right hand)	18
17. Three Octave Arpeggios (left hand)	19
18. Massive Chord Inversions	20
19. Chromatic Octaves	21
20. Chromatic Chord Progressions	22
21. Wide Reaches	23

PRACTICE SUGGESTIONS

To derive the full benefit from these exercises, they should be played with a firm, solid finger action. **Listen carefully while practicing**. Try to play **each finger equally loud**. Each hand should also play equally loud. It is also important to be aware of the feeling in your fingers and hands during practice.

Each exercise should be practiced four or five times daily, starting at a slow tempo and gradually increasing the tempo as proficiency improves. Several previously learned exercises should be reviewed each week as part of regular practice.

Discover an Amazing Variety of Companion Books:

www.schaumpiano.net

The Schaum website contains a description and complete contents of each book:
Methods • Workbooks • Theory • Technic • Repertoire
Christmas • Classics • Duets • Folk Songs • Patriotic • Sacred

Primer Level through Level 6

1. Finger Repetition Study

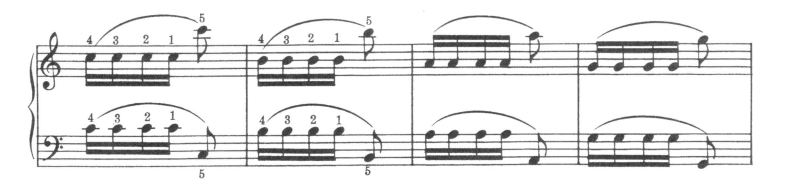

2. Melody and Accompaniment

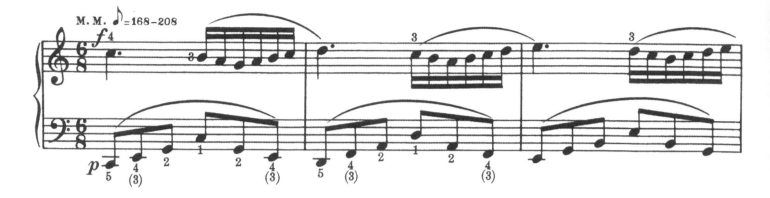

3. Accompaniment and Melody

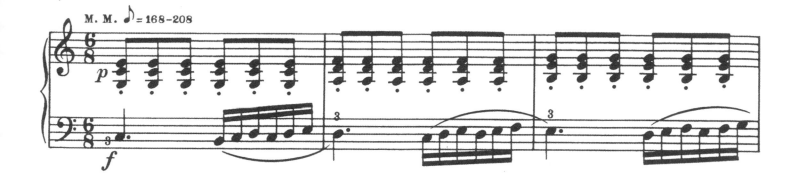

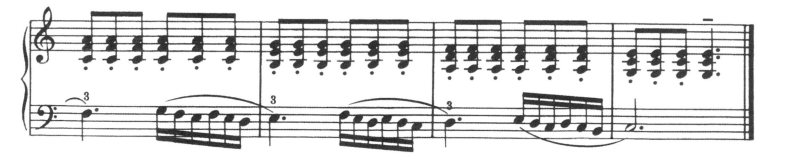

6

4. Modulation (Chords)

M. M. ♩=120–144

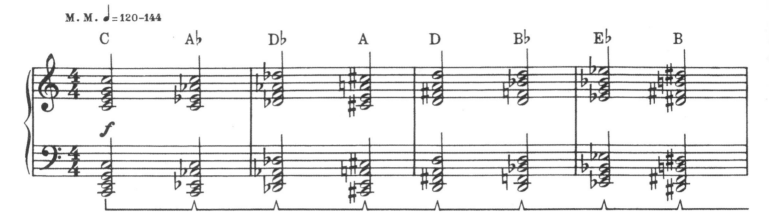

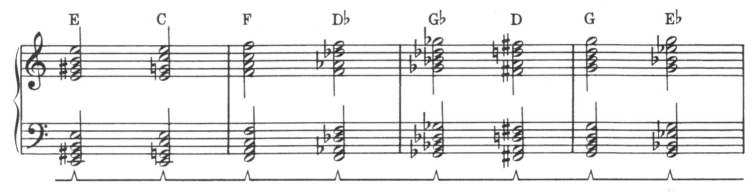

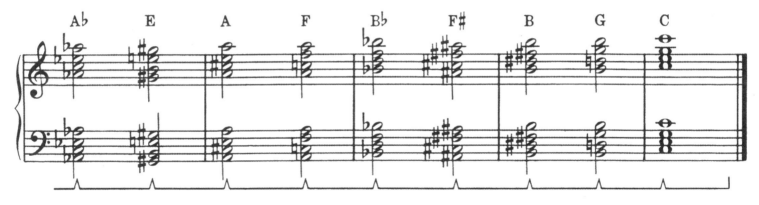

5. Modulation (Arpeggios)

M. M. ♩=120–144

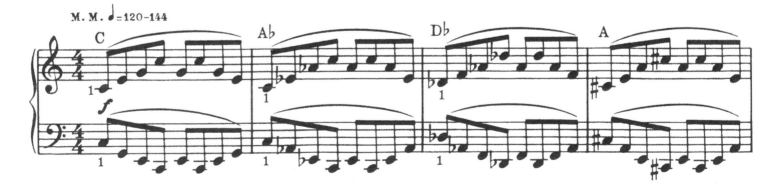

How to Practice
1. Play Modulation Study No. 4 as written
2. Then play Modulation Study No. 5 in blocked chords
3. Play Modulation Study No. 5 as written
4. Then play Modulation Study No. 4 in broken chords

6. Legato Sixths

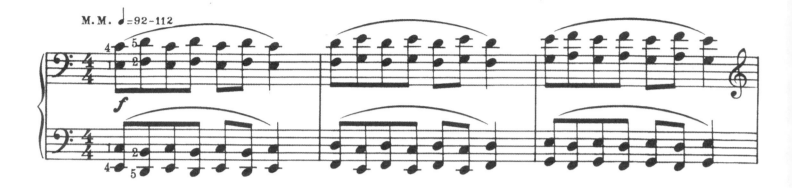

7. Diatonic Octaves

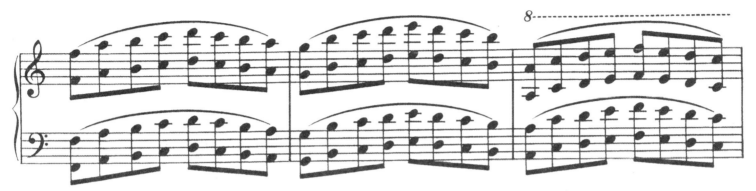

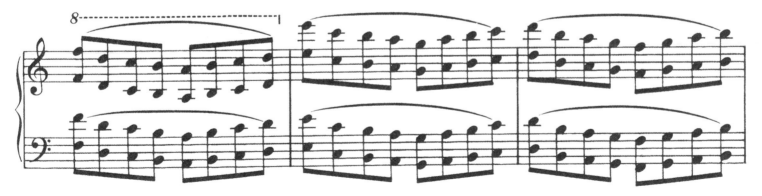

10

8. Broken Octaves (Ascending)

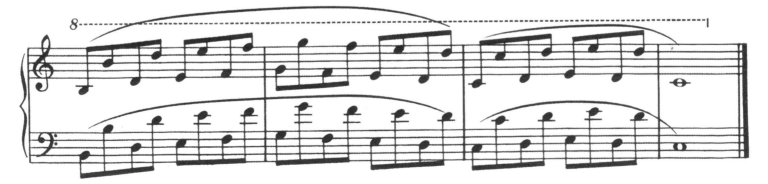

9. Broken Octaves (Descending)

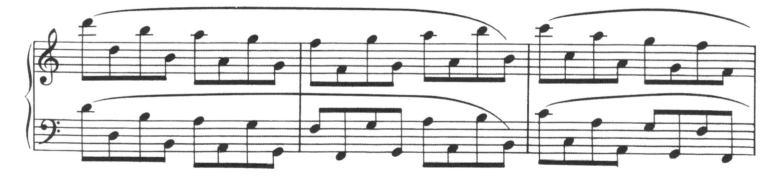

10. Tremolo (Sustained Octaves)

11. Tremolo (Sustained Thirds)

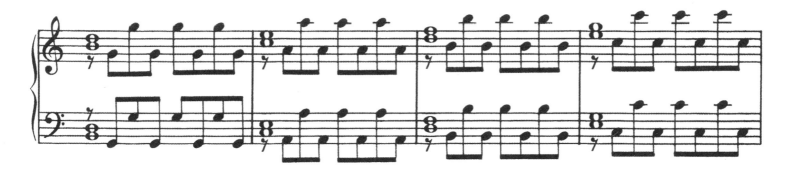

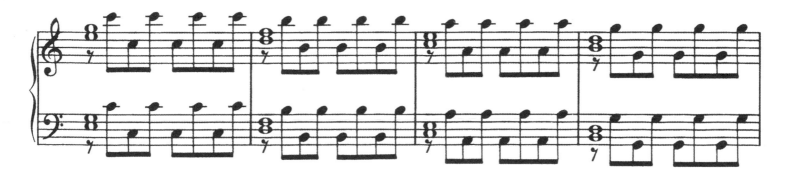

12. Parallel Arpeggios

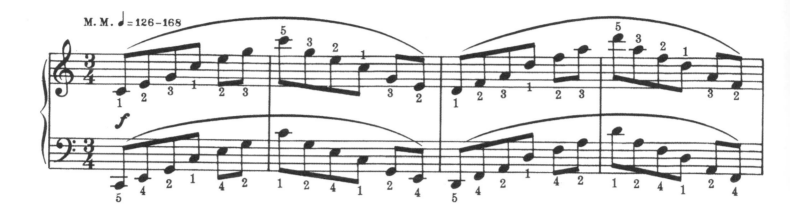

13. Arpeggios in Contrary Motion

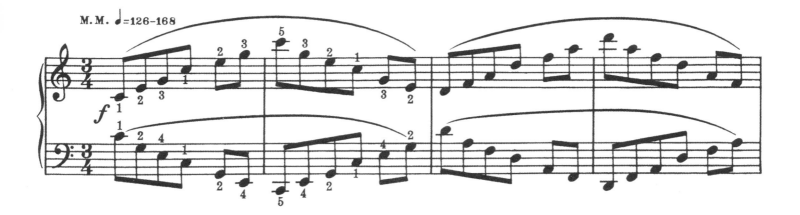

14. Sustained Octaves (Repeated Thirds)

15. Sustained Thirds (Repeated Octaves)

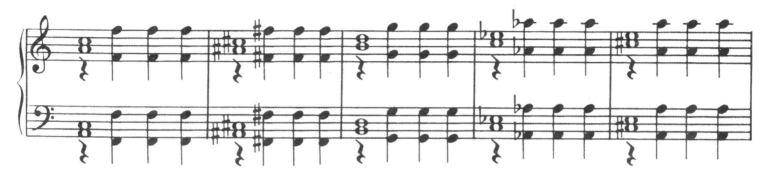

16. Three Octave Arpeggios (Right Hand)

17. Three Octave Arpeggios (Left Hand)

18. Massive Chord Inversions

19. Chromatic Octaves

M. M. ♩ = 100–126

Note: Use 1st and 4th fingers on all black key octaves.

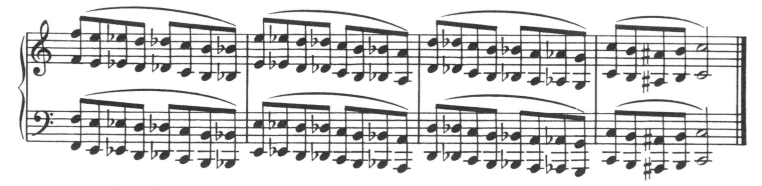

20. Chromatic Chord Progressions

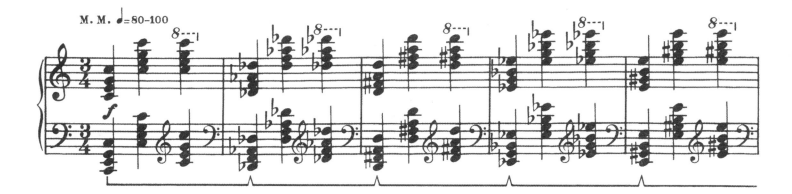

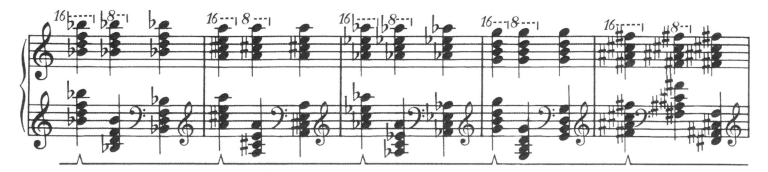

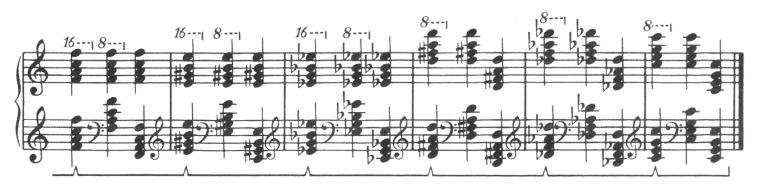

21. Wide Reaches

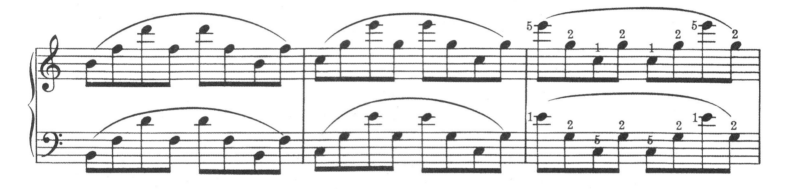

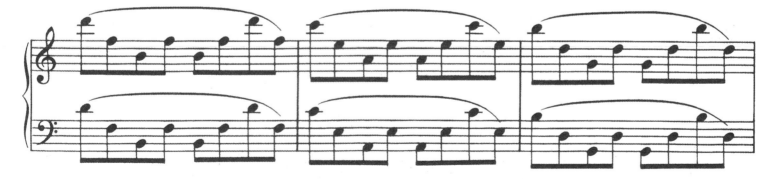

You are now ready to progress to Schaum Fingerpower®, Level Six (0426)